EASY GUITAR
WITH NOTES & TAB

TOP HITS OF 2022

ISBN 978-1-7051-7467-8

HAL•LEONARD®

Visit Hal Leonard Online at
www.halleonard.com

World headquarters, contact:
Hal Leonard
7777 West Bluemound Road
Milwaukee, WI 53213
Email: info@halleonard.com

In Europe, contact:
Hal Leonard Europe Limited
1 Red Place
London, W1K 6PL
Email: info@halleonardeurope.com

In Australia, contact:
Hal Leonard Australia Pty. Ltd.
4 Lentara Court
Cheltenham, Victoria, 3192 Australia
Email: info@halleonard.com.au

STRUM AND PICK PATTERNS

This chart contains the suggested strum and pick patterns that are referred to by number at the beginning of each song in this book. The symbols ⊓ and ∨ in the strum patterns refer to down and up strokes, respectively. The letters in the pick patterns indicate which right-hand fingers play which strings.

p = thumb
i = index finger
m = middle finger
a = ring finger

For example; Pick Pattern 2
is played: thumb - index - middle - ring

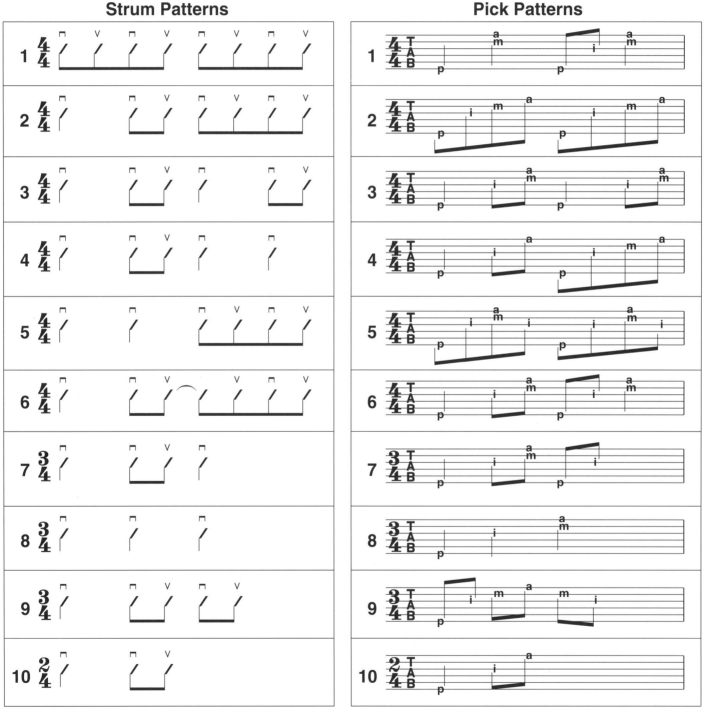

You can use the 3/4 Strum and Pick Patterns in songs written in compound meter (6/8, 9/8, 12/8, etc.). For example, you can accompany a song in 6/8 by playing the 3/4 pattern twice in each measure. The 4/4 Strum and Pick Patterns can be used for songs written in cut time (¢) by doubling the note time values in the patterns. Each pattern would therefore last two measures in cut time.

As It Was

Words and Music by Harry Styles, Thomas Hull and Tyler Johnson

*Capo IX

Strum Pattern: 3, 4
Pick Pattern: 3, 4

Intro
Fast
N.C.

*To match recording, place capo at 9th fret.

Verse

1. Hold-ing me back, _____ grav-i-ty's hold-ing me back. _____ I want you to
2. An-swer the phone, _____ "Har-ry, you're no good a-lone. _____ Why are you

hold out   the palm of   your   hand.   Why don't   we   leave   it   at   that?   _____
sit-ting   at home on   the   floor?   What kind   of   pills   are   you   on?"   _____

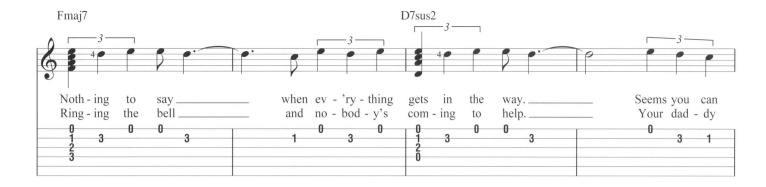

Noth - ing to say _____ when ev - 'ry - thing gets in the way. _____ Seems you can
Ring - ing the bell _____ and no - bod - y's com - ing to help. _____ Your dad - dy

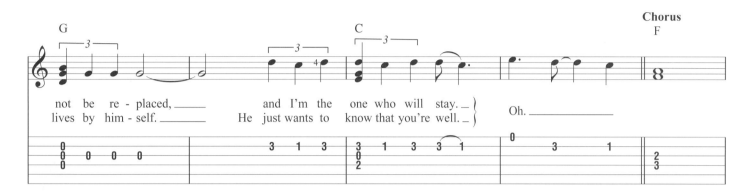

not be re - placed, _____ and I'm the one who will stay. ⎫
lives by him - self. _____ He just wants to know that you're well. ⎭ Oh. _____

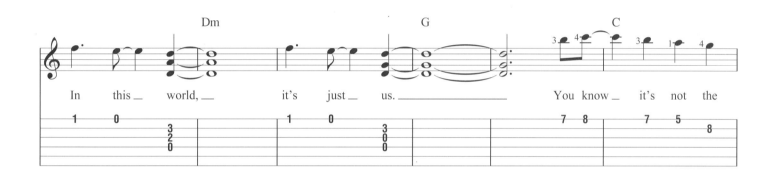

In this ___ world, ___ it's just ___ us. _____ You know ___ it's not the

same as ___ it was. In this ___ world, ___ it's just ___ us. _____ You know ___

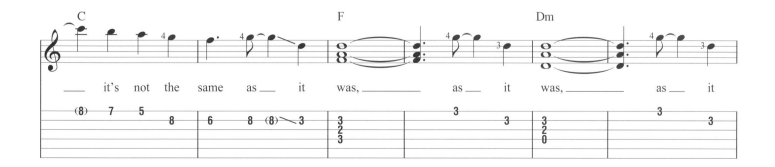

___ it's not the same as ___ it was, _____ as ___ it was, _____ as ___ it

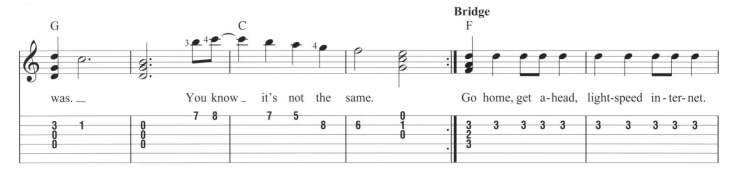

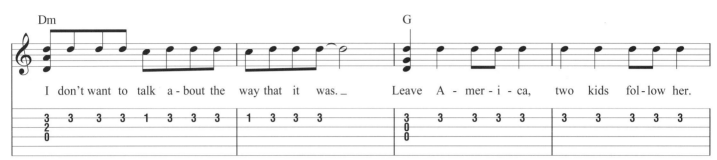

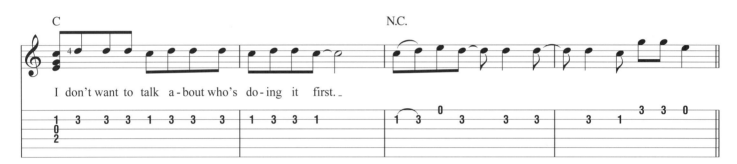

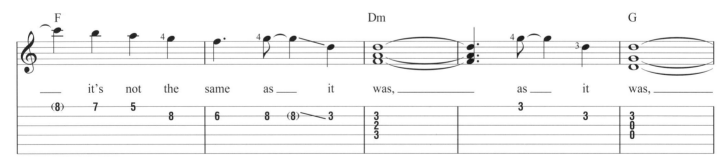

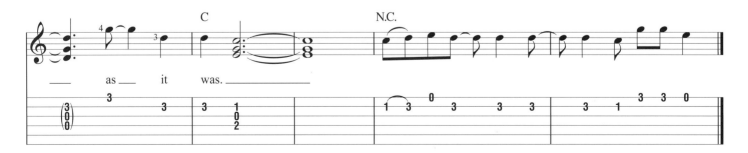

Freedom

Words and Music by Tierce Person, Autumn Rowe, Andrae Alexander and Jonathan Batiste

*Capo V

Strum Pattern: 3, 5

Pick Pattern: 3, 4

Intro

Moderately fast

*To match recording, place capo at 5th fret.

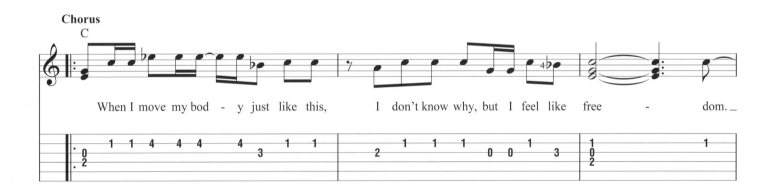

When I move my bod - y just like this, I don't know why, but I feel like free - dom. _

_ I hear a song _ that takes me back, and I let go with so much free - dom. _

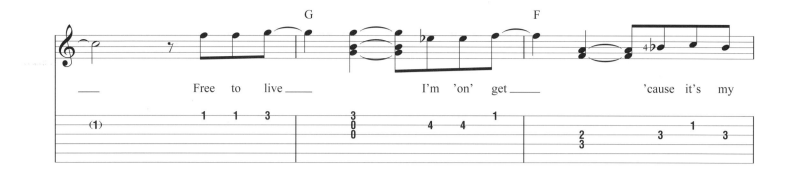

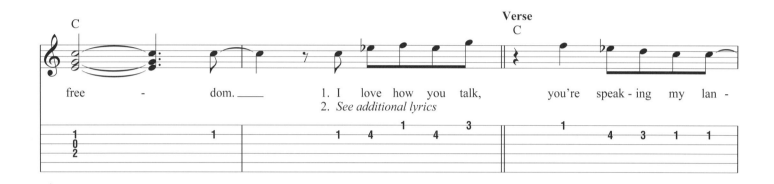

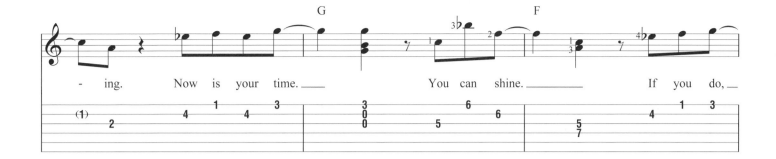

-ing.　Now is your time.＿＿＿　You can shine.＿＿＿　If you do,＿＿＿

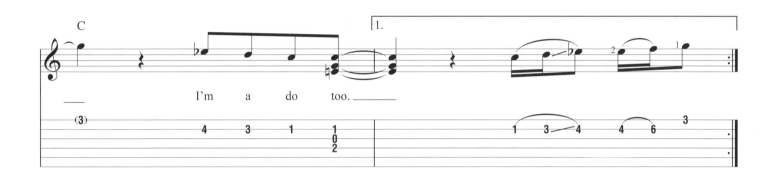

＿＿＿　I'm a do too.＿＿＿＿

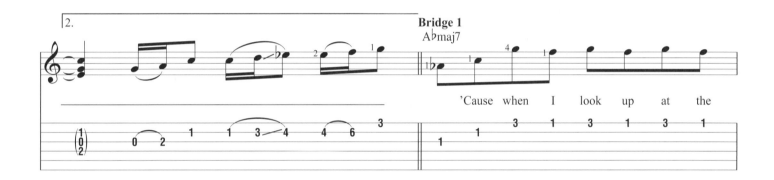

'Cause when I look up at the

stars　I know ex-act-ly who we are,　'cause then I see you shine,　you shin-

*Sung one octave higher.

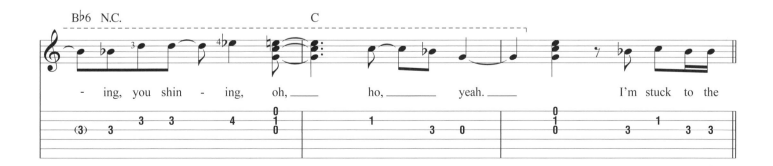

-ing, you shin - ing, oh, ＿＿＿ ho, ＿＿＿ yeah. ＿＿＿ I'm stuck to the

Bridge 2

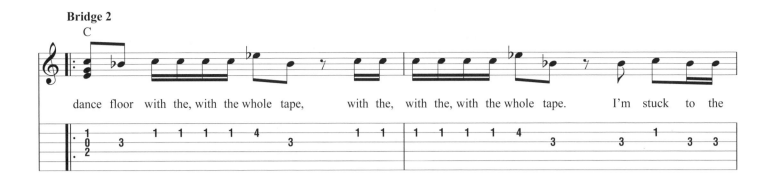

dance floor with the, with the whole tape, with the, with the, with the whole tape. I'm stuck to the

dance floor with the, with the whole tape, with the, with the, with the whole tape. Give you just what you

ask for, giv-in' you the whole shake. I'm a give you the whole shake. I'm stuck to the

dance floor with the, with the whole tape, with the, with the, with the whole tape. I say yeah.

_____ oh yeah,_____ 'cause you do, I'm a do too.___ I'm stuck to the

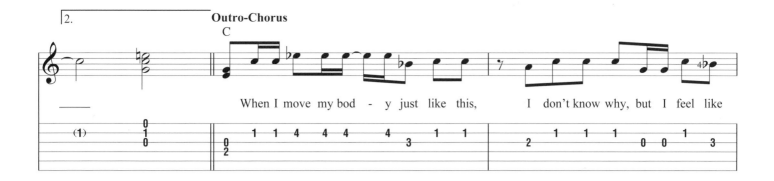

When I move my bod - y just like this, I don't know why, but I feel like

free - dom. _____ I hear a song ___ that takes me back, and I

let go with so much free - dom. ___ Free to live ___ I'm 'on' get ___

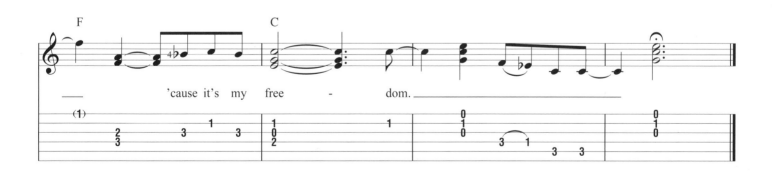

___ 'cause it's my free - dom. _____

Additional Lyrics

2. The reason we get down is to get back up.
   If someone's around, go on, let them look.
   You can't sit still, this ain't no drill.
   More than cheap thrills.
   Now is your time. You can shine.
   If you do, I'm a do too.

Enemy

Words and Music by Daniel Coulter Reynolds, Daniel Wayne Sermon, Benjamin Arthur McKee,
Daniel James Platzman, Justin Tranter, Mattias Larsson and Robin Fredriksson

Strum Pattern: 3
Pick Pattern: 3

Verse
Moderately slow, in 2

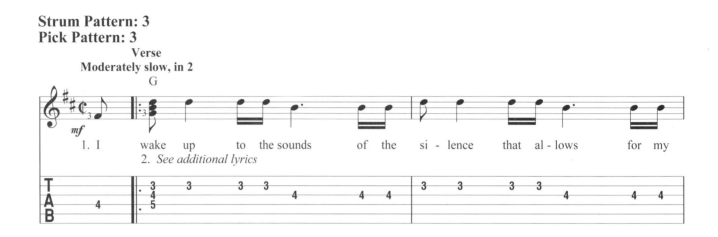

1. I wake up to the sounds of the si-lence that al-lows for my
2. *See additional lyrics*

mind to run a-round with my ear up to the ground. I'm search-ing to be-hold the

stor-ies that are told when my back is to the world that was smil-ing when I turned.

Pre-Chorus

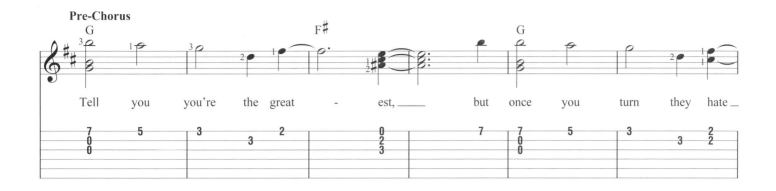

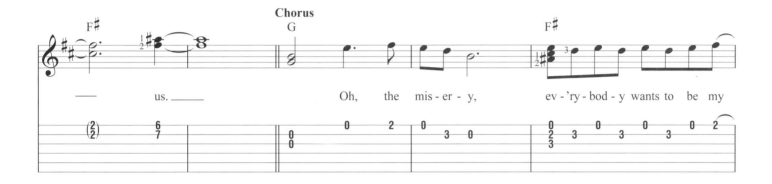

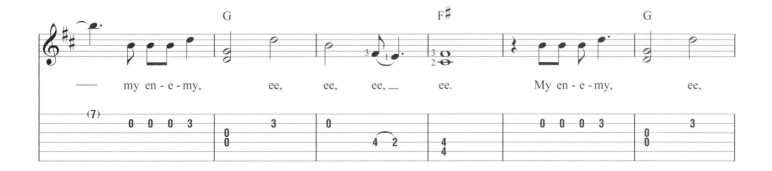

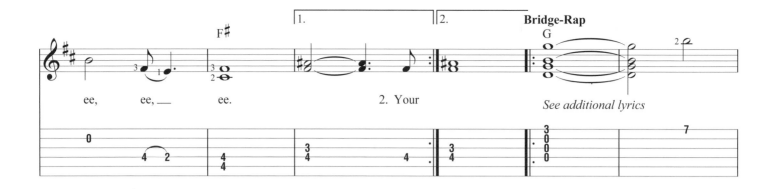

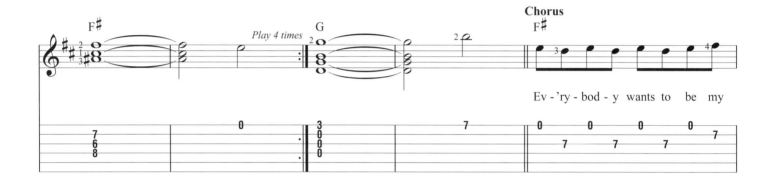

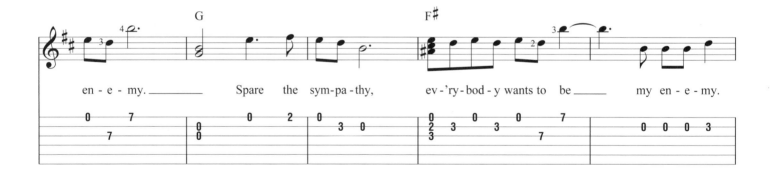

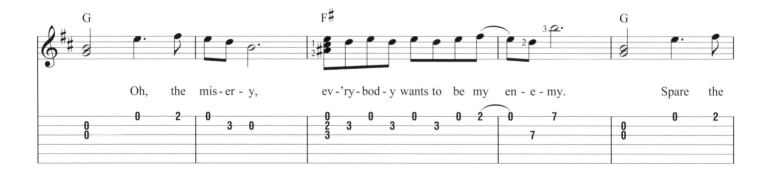

sym-pa-thy,   ev-'ry-bod-y wants to be ____ my en-e-my.   Play a - way,   I swear, I'll nev-er be a

saint, no   way, ____   my en - e - my.   Pray a - way,   I swear, I'll ne-ver be a   saint. _____

Additional Lyrics

2. Your words up on the wall, as you're praying for my fall.
   And the laughter in the halls and the names that I've been called.
   I stack it in my mind and I'm waiting for the time
   When I show you what it's like to be words spit in a mic.

Rap: *Uh, look, okay.*
   I'm hopin' that somebody pray for me.
   I'm prayin' that somebody hope for me.
   I'm stayin' where nobody 'posed to be.
   P-p-posted. Being a wreck of emotions.
   Ready to go whenever, just let me know.
   The road is long, so put the pedal to the floor.
   The enemy is on my trail, my energy unavailable.
   I'm a tell 'em "Hasta luego."
   They wanna plot on my trot to the top.
   I been outta shape thinkin' out the box, I'm an astronaut.
   I blasted off the planet rock to cause catastrophe.
   And it matters more because I had it not.
   Had I thought about wreaking havoc
   On an opposition, kinda shockin' they wanted static
   With precision, I'm automatic quarterback.
   I ain't talkin' sackin', pack it.
   Pack it up, I don't panic, batter-batter up.
   Who the baddest? It don't matter 'cause we're at your throat.

Glimpse of Us

Words and Music by Joji Kusunoki, Connor McDonough, Riley McDonough, Joel Castillo and Alexis Kesselman

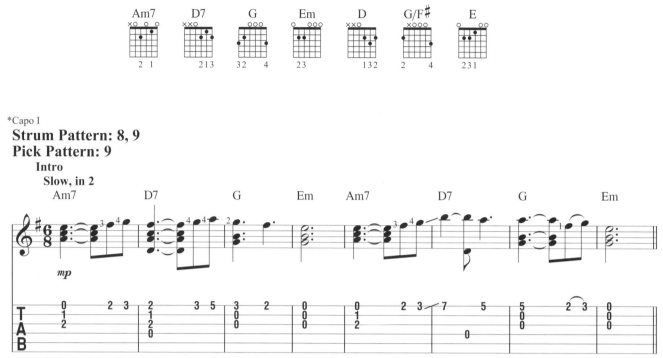

*Capo I

Strum Pattern: 8, 9
Pick Pattern: 9

Intro
Slow, in 2

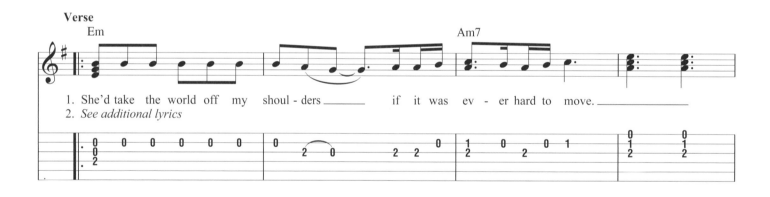

*Optional: To match recording, place capo at 1st fret.

Verse

1. She'd take the world off my shoul-ders _____ if it was ev-er hard to move. _____
2. *See additional lyrics*

She'd turn the rain to a rain-bow _____ when I was liv-ing in the blue. _____

Why then if she's so per - fect ___ do I still wish that it was you? _____

Per - fect don't mean that it's work-ing, so what can I do _____ when you're out of

§ **Chorus**

sight in my mind? ___ 'Cause some - times I look in her eyes, and that's where I

find a glimpse of us. _____ And I try to fall for her touch, but I'm think-ing of the way it

was. _____ Said I'm fine, and said I moved on, I'm on-ly here pass-ing time in her arms, hop-ig I'll

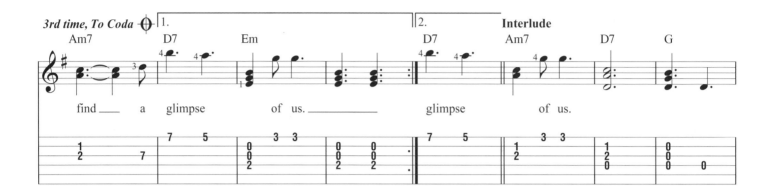

find _____ a glimpse of us. _____ glimpse of us.

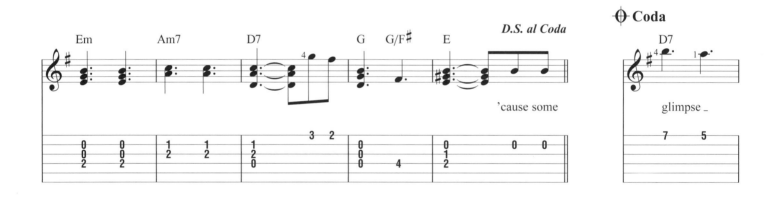

'cause some glimpse _

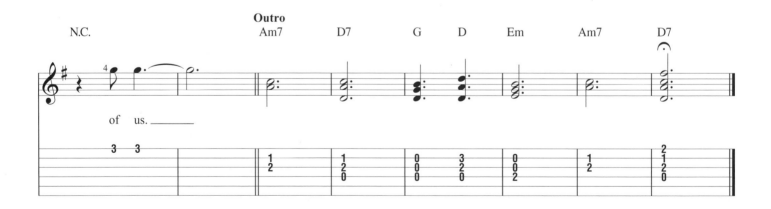

of us. _____

Additional Lyrics

2. Tell me he savors your glory. Does he laugh the way I did?
   Is this the part of your story, one that I had never lived?
   Maybe one day you'll feel lonely, and in his eyes you'll get a glimpse.
   Maybe you'll start slipping slowly and find me again
   When you're out of sight in my mind.

On My Way

from MARRY ME

Words and Music by Leroy James Clampitt, Ivy Adara and Michael Pollack

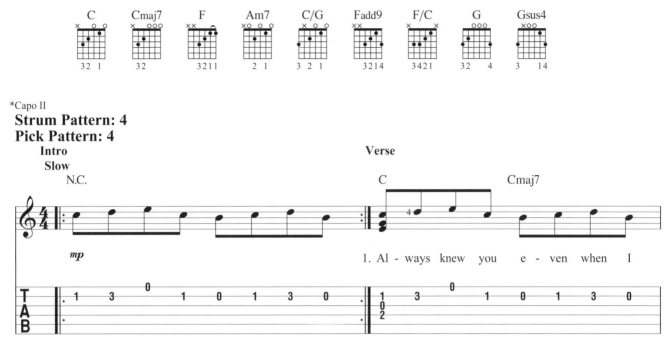

*Capo II

Strum Pattern: 4
Pick Pattern: 4

*Optional: To match recording, place capo at 2nd fret.

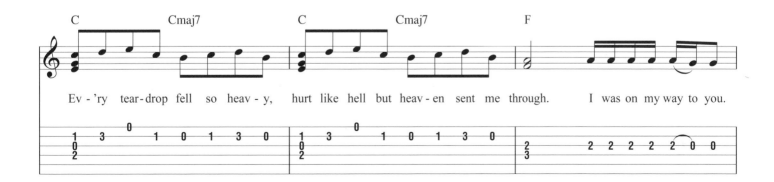

And ev-'ry heart-break was a yel-low brick road

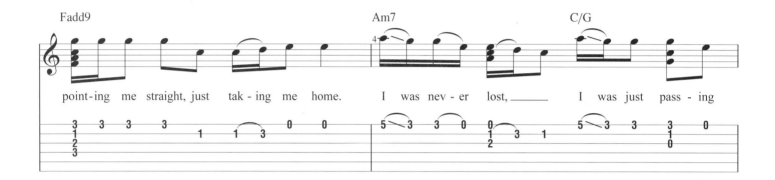

point-ing me straight, just tak-ing me home. I was nev-er lost, _____ I was just pass-ing

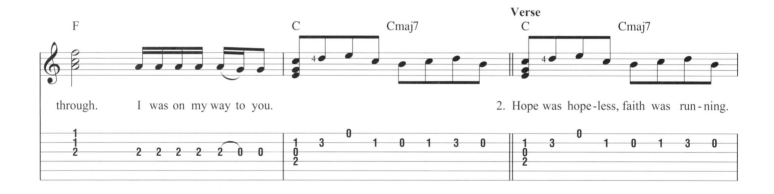

through. I was on my way to you. 2. Hope was hope-less, faith was run-ning.

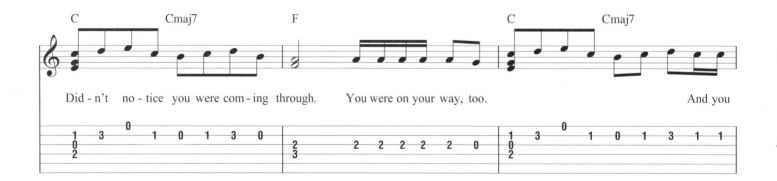

Did-n't no-tice you were com-ing through. You were on your way, too. And you

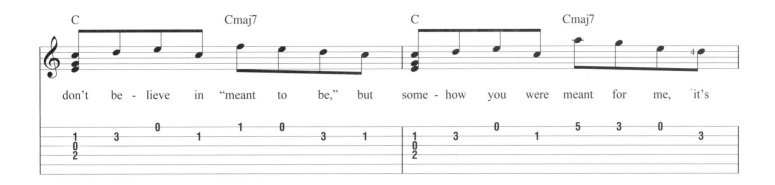

don't be-lieve in "meant to be," but some-how you were meant for me, it's

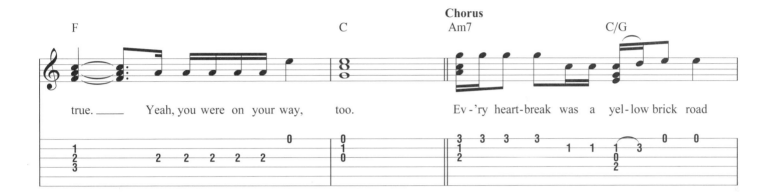

true.____ Yeah, you were on your way, too. Ev-'ry heart-break was a yel-low brick road

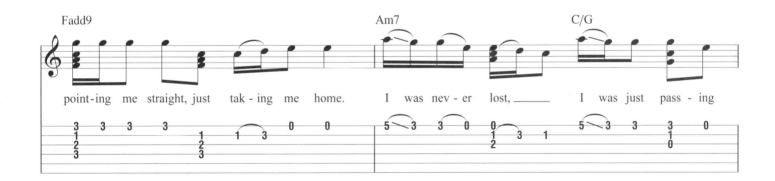

point-ing me straight, just tak-ing me home. I was nev-er lost,____ I was just pass-ing

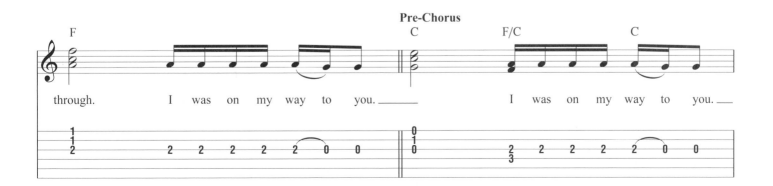

through. I was on my way to you.____ I was on my way to you.____

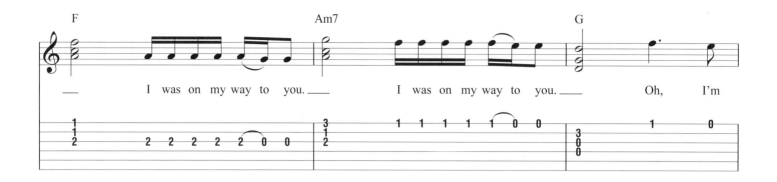

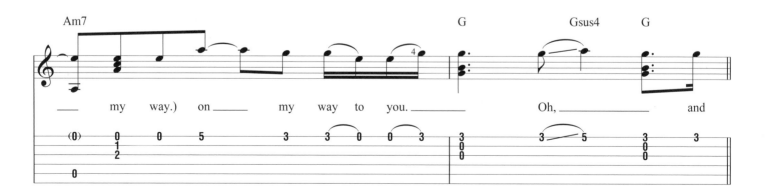

Chorus

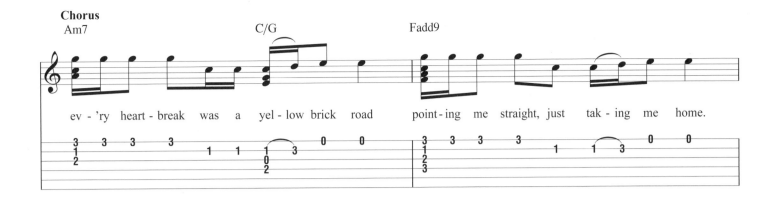

ev-'ry heart-break was a yel-low brick road point-ing me straight, just tak-ing me home.

I was nev-er lost, _____ I was just pass-ing through on _____ my way to you. _____

Outro

_____ Ooh, _____ ooh. _____ On _____ my way to you. _____

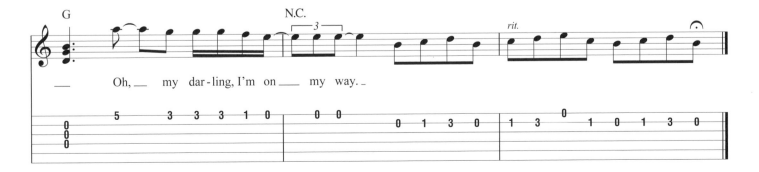

_____ Oh, _____ my dar-ling, I'm on _____ my way. _____

Hold My Hand

from TOP GUN: MAVERICK

Words and Music by Stefani Germanotta and Michael Tucker

*Capo VII

Strum Pattern: 8, 9
Pick Pattern: 7, 8

*To match recording, place capo at 7th fret.

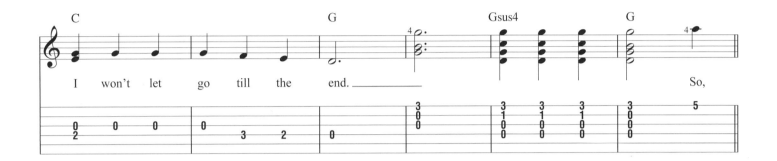

Chorus

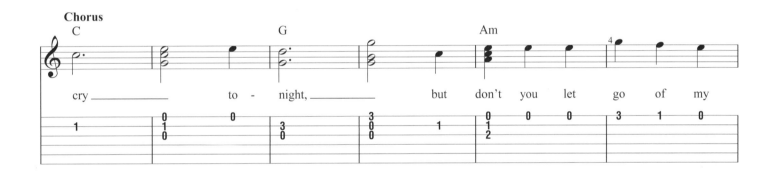

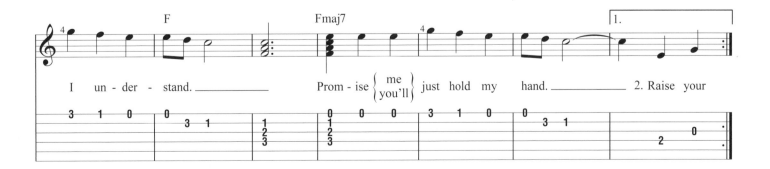

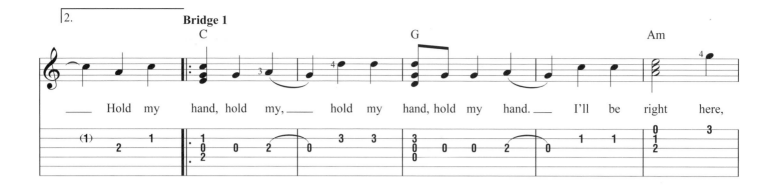

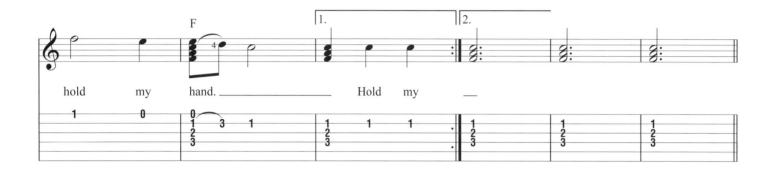

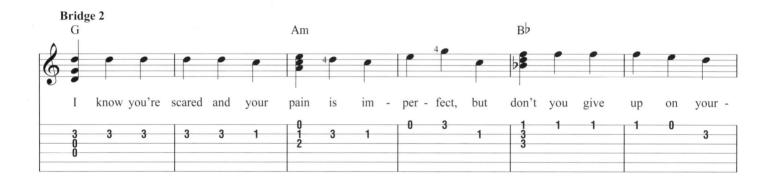

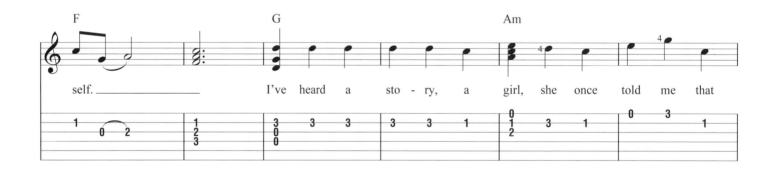

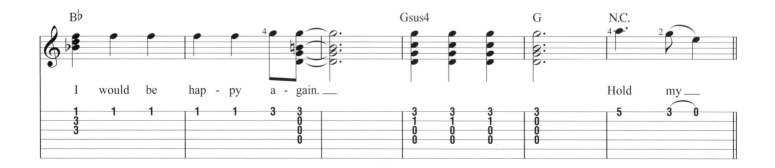

Outro

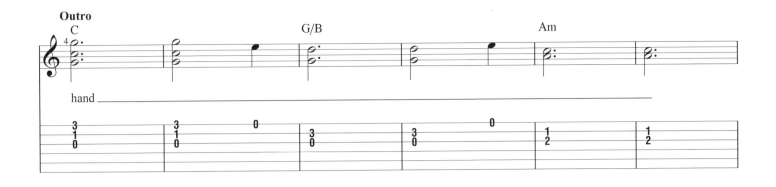

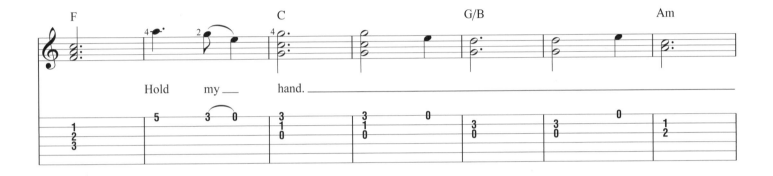

Nobody Like U

from TURNING RED

Music and Lyrics by Billie Eilish and Finneas O'Connell

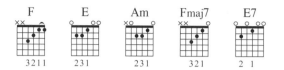

Strum Pattern: 3, 4
Pick Pattern: 3, 4

Intro
Moderately fast

1. I've nev-er met no-

Verse

bod-y ____ like you. Had friends and I've had bud-dies, ____ it's true. ___ But they don't turn my

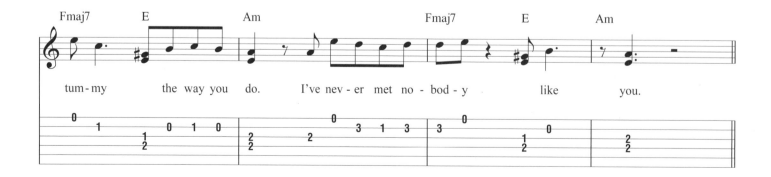

tum-my the way you do. I've nev-er met no-bod-y like you.

Interlude

You're nev-er not on my

Chorus

mind, oh my, oh my. I'm nev-er not by your side, your side, your side. I'm nev-er gon-na let you

cry, oh cry, don't cry. I'll nev-er not be your ride or die, al - right.

Interlude/Rap

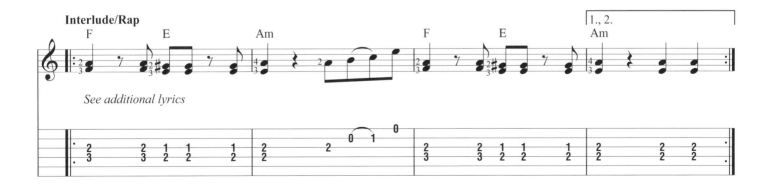

See additional lyrics

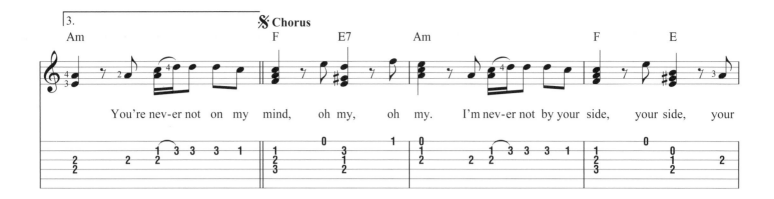

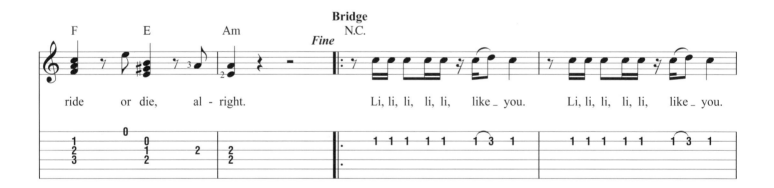

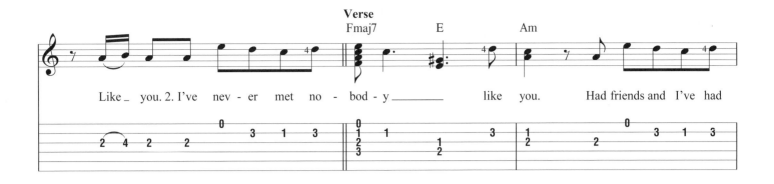

Like _ you. 2. I've nev - er met no - bod - y _____ like you. Had friends and I've had

bud - dies, _____ it's true. _ But they don't turn my tum - my _____ the way you

D.S. al Fine

do. I've nev - er met no - bod - y _____ like _ you. You're nev - er not on my

Additional Lyrics

Rap: Let's call it what it is, it's a masterpiece.
Got a whole lotta love for them city streets.
Glendale tonight is the place to be.
Got a big boom box and a new CD.
Come on everybody let's tear it up.
If you want mad skills, you can share with us.
I want everybody to stop and stare.
And you know why, it's me, Robaire.
Woo, uhh, let's go.

Numb Little Bug

Words and Music by Emily Beihold, Nicholas Lopez and Andrew DeCaro

*Capo IV

Strum Pattern: 3
Pick Pattern: 3

Intro
Moderately slow

*Optional: To match recording, place capo at 4th fret.

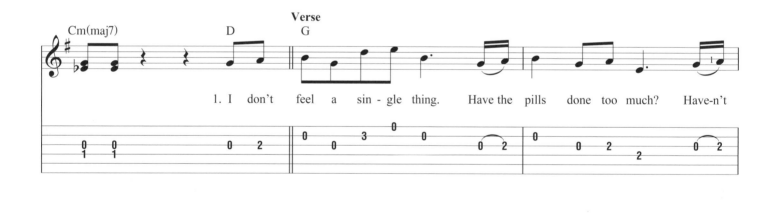

1. I don't feel a sin-gle thing. Have the pills done too much? Have-n't caught up with my friends in weeks and now __ we're out-ta touch. I've been driv-in' in L. A. and the

love but it's been in the air? Am I past _ re - pair? ____ A lit-tle bit tired _ of

Bridge

try'n' to care when I don't. ____ A lit-tle bit tired _ of quick re - pairs to

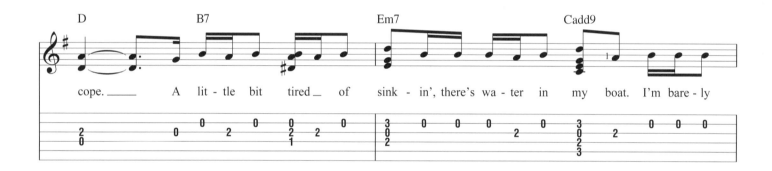

cope. ____ A lit-tle bit tired _ of sink - in', there's wa - ter in my boat. I'm bare - ly

To Coda ⊕

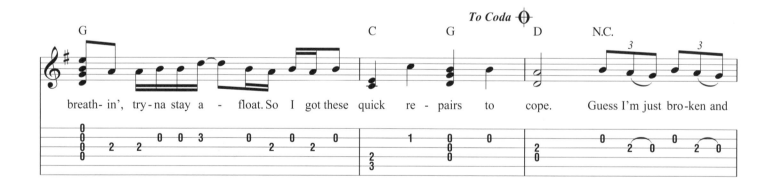

breath-in', try-na stay a - float. So I got these quick re - pairs to cope. Guess I'm just bro-ken and

Verse

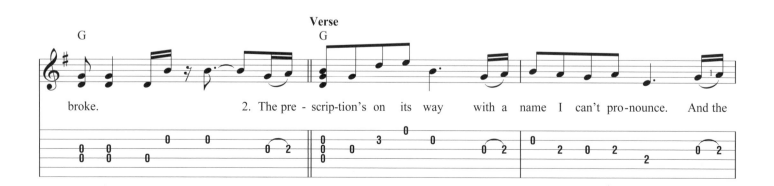

broke. 2. The pre - scrip-tion's on its way with a name I can't pro-nounce. And the

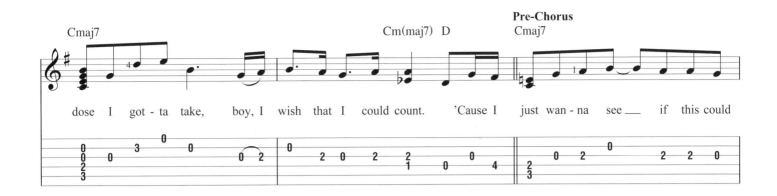

dose I got-ta take, boy, I wish that I could count. 'Cause I just wan-na see ___ if this could

make me hap - py. ___ Do you ev - er get a

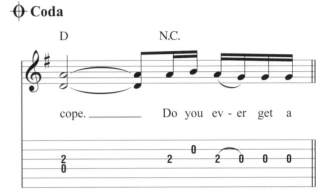

cope. ___ Do you ev - er get a

lit - tle bit tired of life? Like you're not ___ real - ly hap - py but you don't wa - na die? Like a numb ___ lit - tle

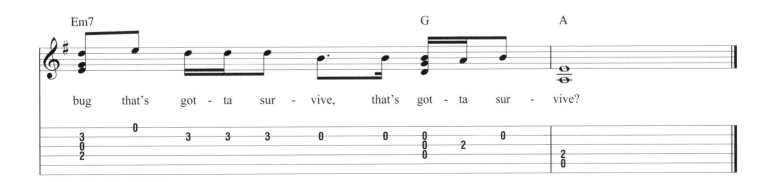

bug that's got - ta sur - vive, that's got - ta sur - vive?

Running Up That Hill

featured in the fourth season of the Netflix series STRANGER THINGS

Words and Music by Kate Bush

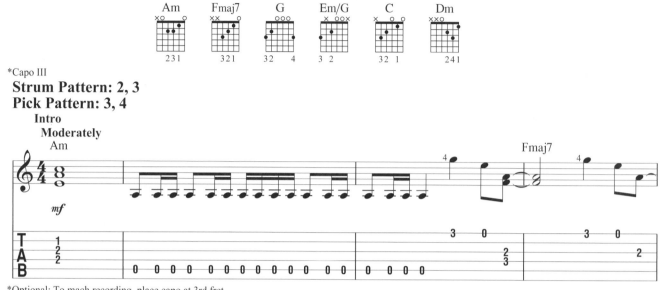

*Capo III

Strum Pattern: 2, 3
Pick Pattern: 3, 4

Intro
Moderately

*Optional: To mach recording, place capo at 3rd fret.

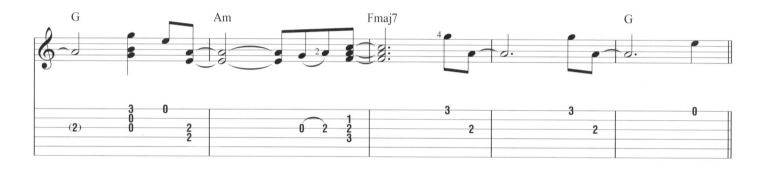

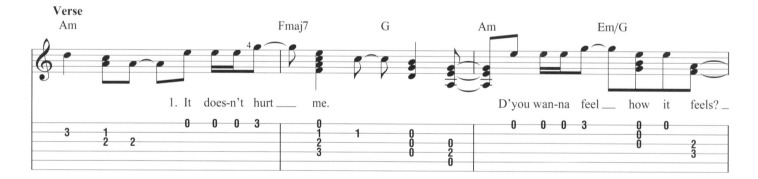

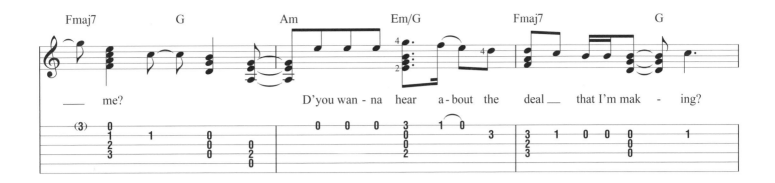

— me? D'you wan-na hear a-bout the deal __ that I'm mak - ing?

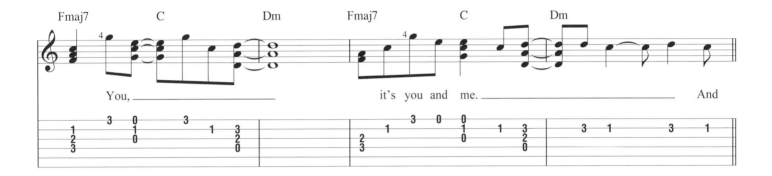

You, _____ it's you and me. _____ And

𝄋 Chorus

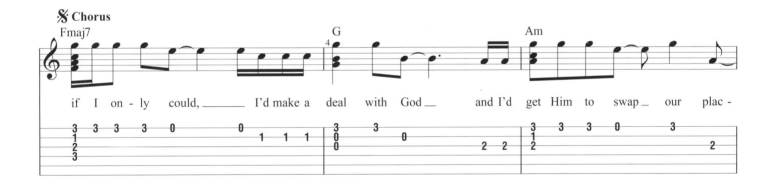

if I on-ly could, _____ I'd make a deal with God __ and I'd get Him to swap __ our plac -

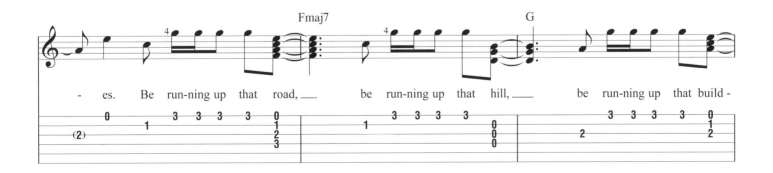

-es. Be run-ning up that road, __ be run-ning up that hill, __ be run-ning up that build -

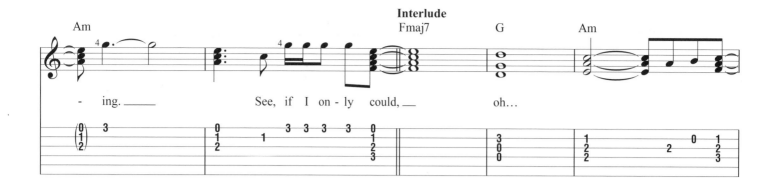

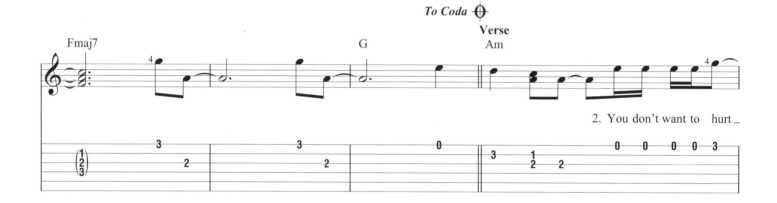

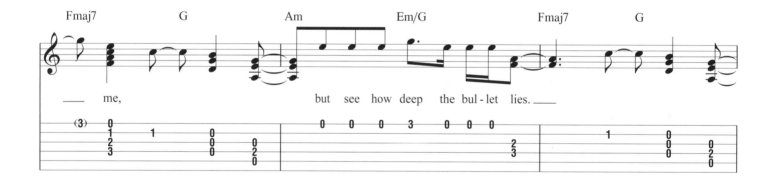

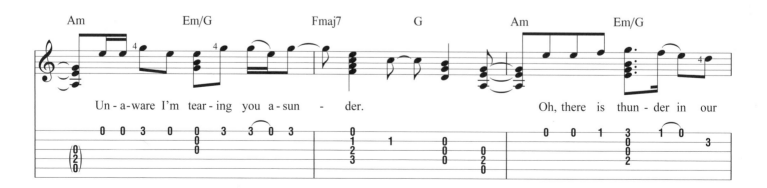

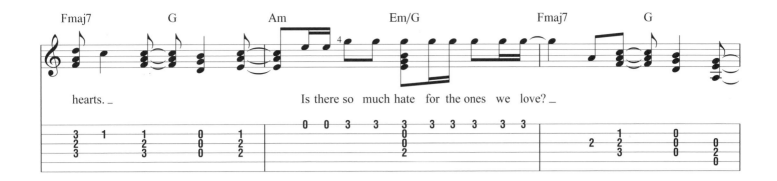

hearts. _ Is there so much hate for the ones we love? _

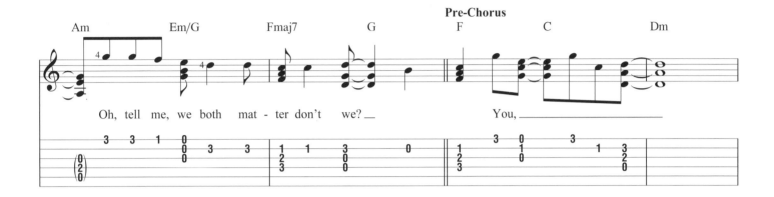

Oh, tell me, we both mat - ter don't we? _ **Pre-Chorus** You, _____

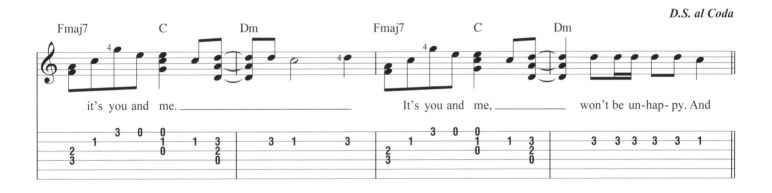

D.S. al Coda

it's you and me. _____ It's you and me, _____ won't be un-hap- py. And

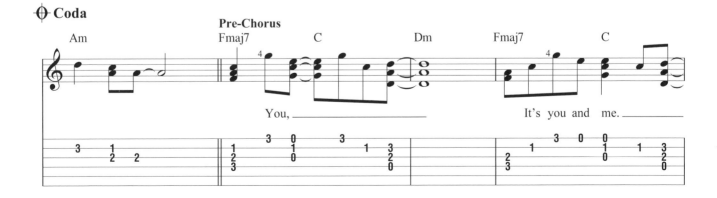

Coda

Pre-Chorus

You, _____ It's you and me. _____

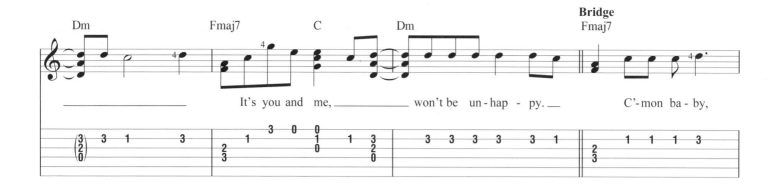

It's you and me, _____ won't be un - hap - py. ___ C'-mon ba - by,

c'-mon dar - ling. Let me steal this mo-ment from you now. C'-mon an - gel,

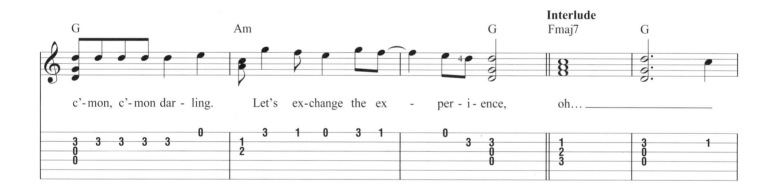

c'-mon, c'-mon dar - ling. Let's ex-change the ex - per - i - ence, oh... _____

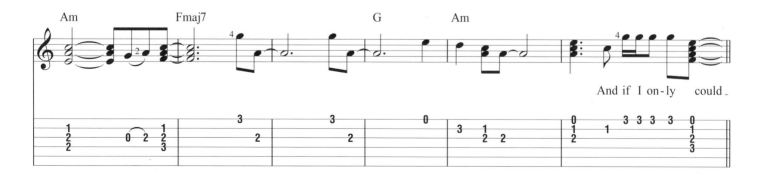

And if I on-ly could _

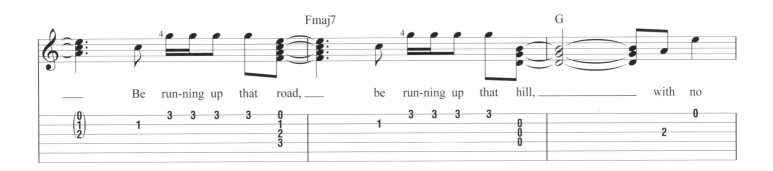

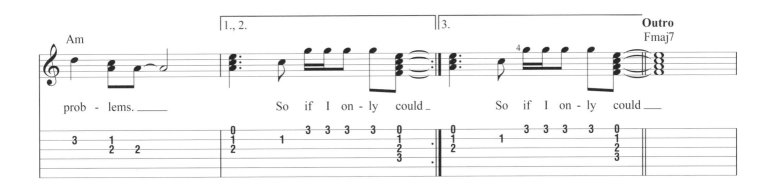

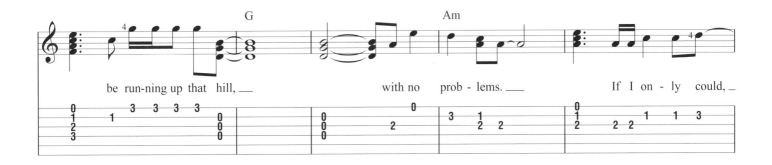

'Til You Can't

Words and Music by Ben Stennis and Matt Rogers

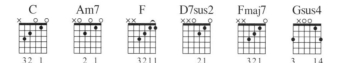

*Capo I

Strum Pattern: 4, 6

Pick Pattern: 2, 4

Intro

Moderately, in 2

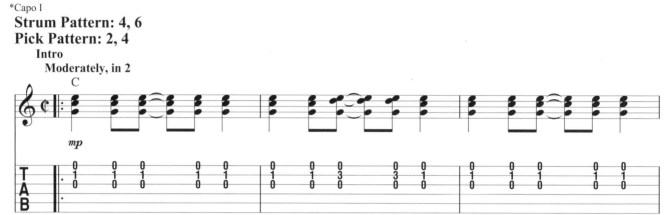

*Optional: To match recording, place capo at 1st fret.

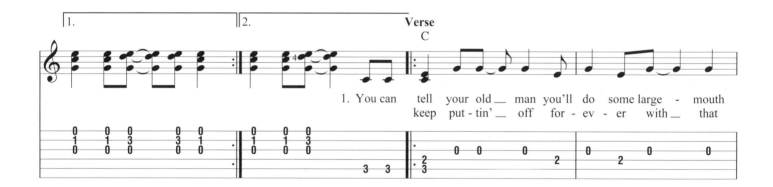

1. You can tell your old __ man you'll do some large - mouth
keep put - tin' __ off for - ev - er with __ that

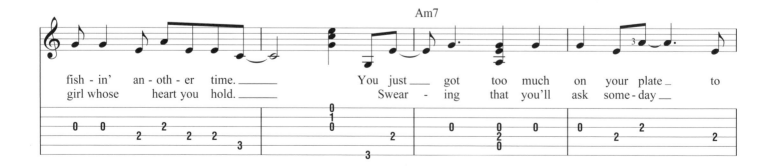

fish - in' an - oth - er time. __ You just __ got too much on your plate __ to
girl whose heart you hold. _____ Swear - ing that you'll ask some - day __

bait and cast ___ a line. ___ You can al - ways put a rain ___ check in his hand ___
fur - ther down ___ the road. ___ You can al - ways put a dia - mond on her hand ___

Interlude

'til you can't.
'til you can't.

1.   2.
2. You can   If you get a chance, ___

𝄋 Chorus

take ___ it, ___ take ___ it while you've got a chance. ___ If you've got a dream, ___

chase ___ it ___ 'cause a dream ___ won't chase you back. ___ If you're gon - na love ___

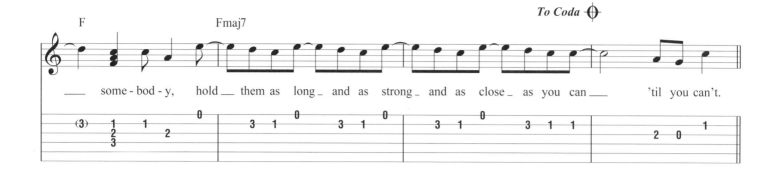

_____ some-bod - y, hold _____ them as long _____ and as strong _____ and as close _____ as you can _____ 'til you can't.

Interlude **Verse**

3. There's a box of greas - y parts _____

_____ sit - tin' in the trunk _____ of that six - ty - five. _____ Still wait - in' on you and your _____

_____ grand - dad _____ to bring it back _____ to life. _____ You can al - ways get a - round _____ to fix - in'

D.S. al Coda

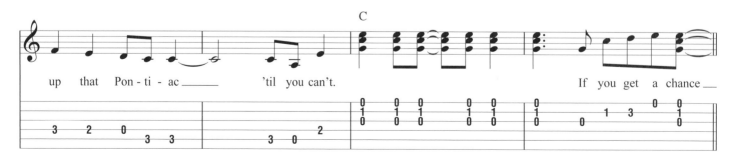

up that Pon - ti - ac _____ 'til you can't. If you get a chance _____

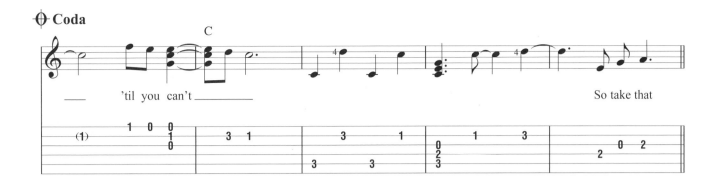

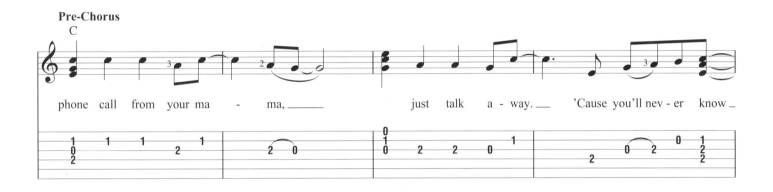

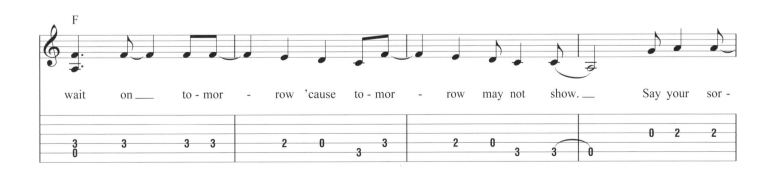

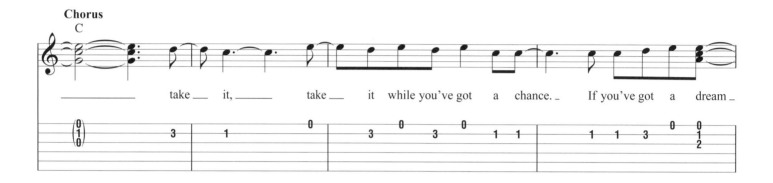

Outro-Chorus

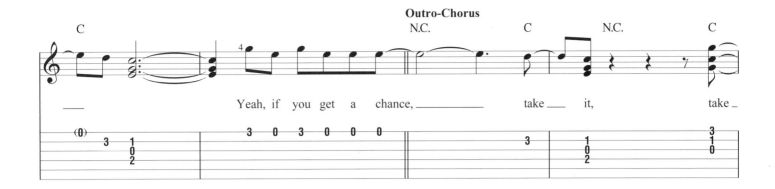

Yeah, if you get a chance, _____ take ___ it, take _

___ it while you've got a chance. _ If you've got a dream, _____ chase _ it, ___ 'cause a dream _

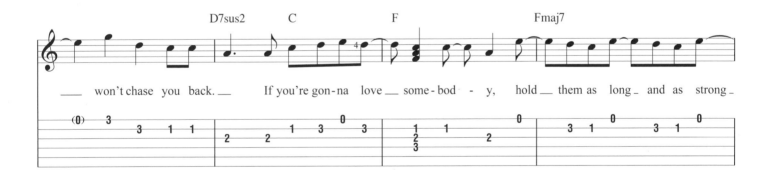

___ won't chase you back. _ If you're gon-na love ___ some-bod - y, hold ___ them as long _ and as strong _

___ and as close _ as you can ___ un - til you can't.   Take it.

Until I Found You

Words and Music by Emily Beihold and Stephen Sanchez

*Capo III

Strum Pattern: 8
Pick Pattern: 8

Intro

Slow, in 4

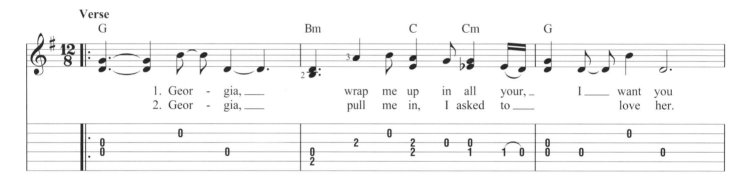

*Optional: To match recording, place capo at 3rd fret.

Verse

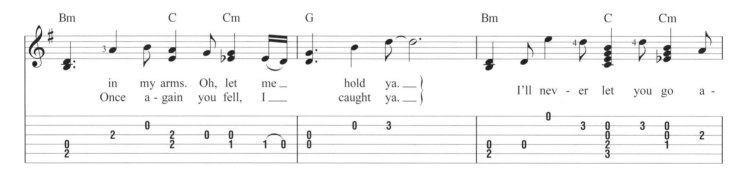

1. Geor - gia, ___ wrap me up in all your, ___ I ___ want you
2. Geor - gia, ___ pull me in, I asked to ___ love her.

in my arms. Oh, let me ___ hold ya. ___ } I'll nev - er let you go a -
Once a - gain you fell, I ___ caught ya. ___ }

Chorus

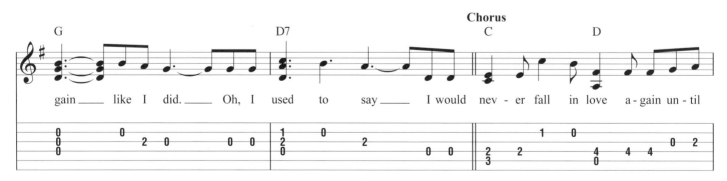

gain ___ like I did. ___ Oh, I used to say ___ I would nev - er fall in love a - gain un - til

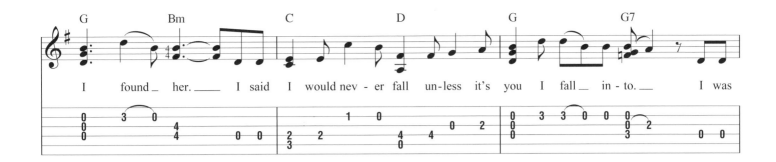

I found her. I said I would nev-er fall un-less it's you I fall in-to. I was

To Coda ⊕

lost with-in the dark-ness, but then I found her. I found you.

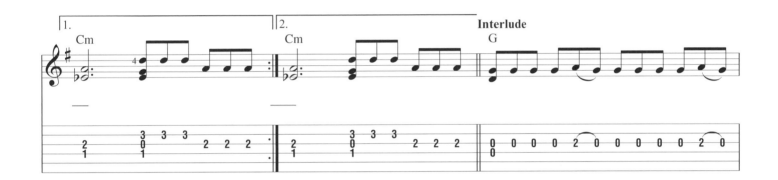

1. | 2. | **Interlude**

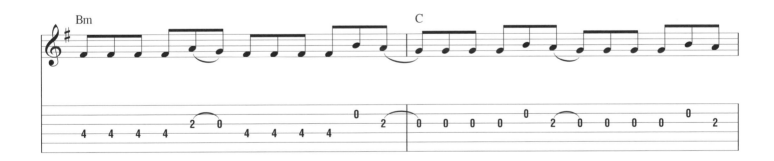

D.S. al Coda

I would

⊕ **Coda**

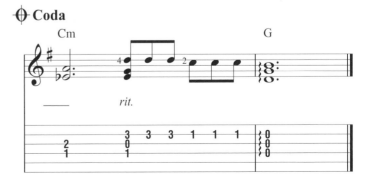

rit.

Wasted on You

Words and Music by Ryan Vojtesak, Josh Thompson, Ernest Smith and Morgan Wallen

*Capo II

Strum Pattern: 8
Pick Pattern: 8

*Optional: To match recording, place capo at 2nd fret.

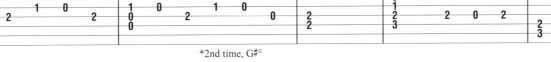

*2nd time, G#°

head and these boots on my feet. Looks like I'm learn-ing the hard way a - gain. That's why I've

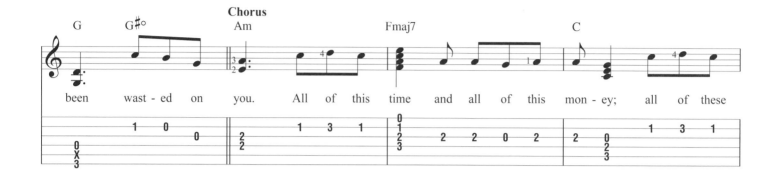

been wast-ed on you. All of this time and all of this mon-ey; all of these

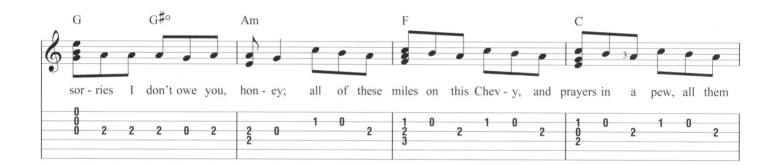

sor - ries I don't owe you, hon - ey; all of these miles on this Chev - y, and prayers in a pew, all them

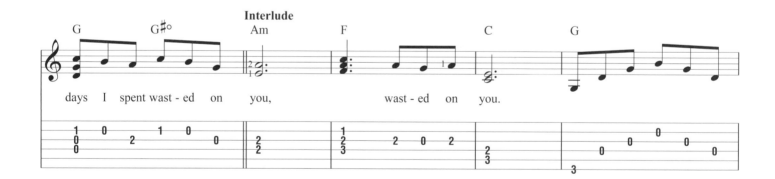

days I spent wast-ed on you, wast-ed on you.

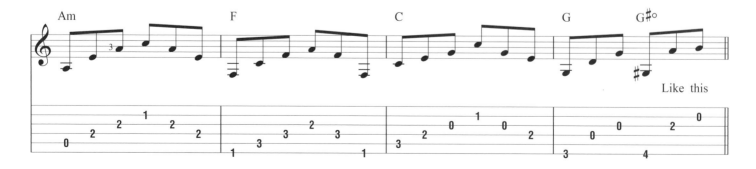

Like this

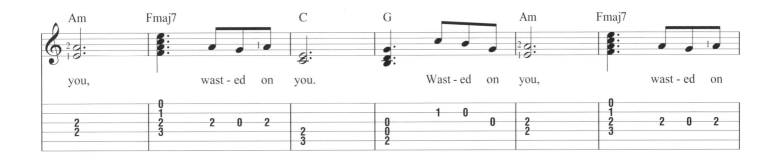

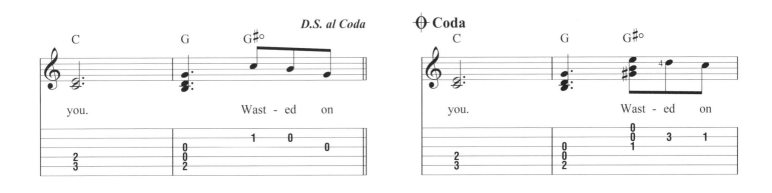

Get Better at Guitar

...with these Great Guitar Instruction Books from Hal Leonard!

101 GUITAR TIPS
INCLUDES TAB

STUFF ALL THE PROS KNOW AND USE

by Adam St. James

This book contains invaluable guidance on everything from scales and music theory to truss rod adjustments, proper recording studio set-ups, and much more.

00695737 Book/Online Audio $17.99

AMAZING PHRASING
INCLUDES TAB

by Tom Kolb

This book/audio pack explores all the main components necessary for crafting well-balanced rhythmic and melodic phrases. It also explains how these phrases are put together to form cohesive solos. The companion audio contains 89 demo tracks, most with full-band backing.

00695583 Book/Online Audio $22.99

ARPEGGIOS FOR THE MODERN GUITARIST
INCLUDES TAB

by Tom Kolb

Using this no-nonsense book with online audio, guitarists will learn to apply and execute all types of arpeggio forms using a variety of techniques, including alternate picking, sweep picking, tapping, string skipping, and legato.

00695862 Book/Online Audio $22.99

BLUES YOU CAN USE
INCLUDES VIDEO/TAB

by John Ganapes

This comprehensive source for learning blues guitar is designed to develop both your lead and rhythm playing. Includes: 21 complete solos • blues chords, progressions and riffs • turnarounds • movable scales and soloing techniques • string bending • utilizing the entire fingerboard • and more.

00142420 Book/Online Media................................$22.99

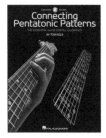

CONNECTING PENTATONIC PATTERNS
INCLUDES TAB

by Tom Kolb

If you've been finding yourself trapped in the pentatonic box, this book is for you! This hands-on book with online audio offers examples for guitar players of all levels, from beginner to advanced. Study this book faithfully, and soon you'll be soloing all over the neck with the greatest of ease.

00696445 Book/Online Audio $24.99

FRETBOARD MASTERY
INCLUDES TAB

by Troy Stetina

Untangle the mysterious regions of the guitar fretboard and unlock your potential. This book familiarizes you with all the shapes you need to know by applying them in real musical examples, thereby reinforcing and reaffirming your newfound knowledge.

00695331 Book/Online Audio $22.99

GUITAR AEROBICS
INCLUDES TAB

by Troy Nelson

Here is a daily dose of guitar "vitamins" to keep your chops fine tuned! Musical styles include rock, blues, jazz, metal, country, and funk. Techniques taught include alternate picking, arpeggios, sweep picking, string skipping, legato, string bending, and rhythm guitar.

00695946 Book/Online Audio $24.99

GUITAR CLUES
INCLUDES TAB

OPERATION PENTATONIC

by Greg Koch

Whether you're new to improvising or have been doing it for a while, this book/audio pack will provide loads of delicious licks and tricks that you can use right away, from volume swells and chicken pickin' to intervallic and chordal ideas.

00695827 Book/Online Audio $19.99

PAT METHENY – GUITAR ETUDES
INCLUDES TAB

Over the years, in many master classes and workshops around the world, Pat has demonstrated the kind of daily workout he puts himself through. This book includes a collection of 14 guitar etudes he created to help you limber up, improve picking technique and build finger independence.

00696587..$17.99

PICTURE CHORD ENCYCLOPEDIA

This comprehensive guitar chord resource for all playing styles and levels features five voicings of 44 chord qualities for all twelve keys – 2,640 chords in all! For each, there is a clearly illustrated chord frame, as well as *an actual photo* of the chord being played!.

00695224..$22.99

RHYTHM GUITAR 365
INCLUDES TAB

by Troy Nelson

This book provides 365 exercises – one for every day of the year! – to keep your rhythm chops fine tuned. Topics covered include: chord theory; the fundamentals of rhythm; fingerpicking; strum patterns; diatonic and non-diatonic progressions; triads; major and minor keys; and more.

00103627 Book/Online Audio $27.99

SCALE CHORD RELATIONSHIPS
INCLUDES TAB

by Michael Mueller & Jeff Schroedl

This book/audio pack explains how to: recognize keys • analyze chord progressions • use the modes • play over nondiatonic harmony • use harmonic and melodic minor scales • use symmetrical scales • incorporate exotic scales • and much more!

00695563 Book/Online Audio $17.99

SPEED MECHANICS FOR LEAD GUITAR
INCLUDES TAB

by Troy Stetina

Take your playing to the stratosphere with this advanced lead book which will help you develop speed and precision in today's explosive playing styles. Learn the fastest ways to achieve speed and control, secrets to make your practice time really count, and how to open your ears and make your musical ideas more solid and tangible.

00699323 Book/Online Audio $22.99

TOTAL ROCK GUITAR
INCLUDES TAB

by Troy Stetina

This comprehensive source for learning rock guitar is designed to develop both your lead and rhythm playing. It covers: getting a tone that rocks • open chords, power chords and barre chords • riffs, scales and licks • string bending, strumming, and harmonics • and more.

00695246 Book/Online Audio $22.99

Guitar World Presents
INCLUDES TAB
STEVE VAI'S GUITAR WORKOUT

In this book, Steve Vai reveals his path to virtuoso enlightenment with two challenging guitar workouts – one 10-hour and one 30-hour – which include scale and chord exercises, ear training, sight-reading, music theory, and much more.

00119643..$16.99

HAL•LEONARD®

Prices, contents, and availability subject to change without notice.

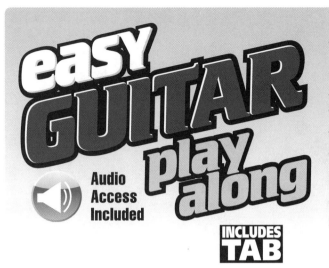

easy GUITAR play along

Audio Access Included

INCLUDES TAB

The *Easy Guitar Play Along*® series features streamlined transcriptions of your favorite songs. Just follow the tab, listen to the audio to hear how the guitar should sound, and then play along using the backing tracks. Playback tools are provided for slowing down the tempo without changing pitch and looping challenging parts. The melody and lyrics are included in the book so that you can sing or simply follow along.

1. ROCK CLASSICS

Jailbreak • Living After Midnight • Mississippi Queen • Rocks Off • Runnin' Down a Dream • Smoke on the Water • Strutter • Up Around the Bend.

00702560 Book/CD Pack....... $14.99

2. ACOUSTIC TOP HITS

About a Girl • I'm Yours • The Lazy Song • The Scientist • 21 Guns • Upside Down • What I Got • Wonderwall.

00702569 Book/CD Pack....... $14.99

3. ROCK HITS

All the Small Things • Best of You • Brain Stew (The Godzilla Remix) • Californication • Island in the Sun • Plush • Smells Like Teen Spirit • Use Somebody.

00702570 Book/CD Pack....... $14.99

4. ROCK 'N' ROLL

Blue Suede Shoes • I Get Around • I'm a Believer • Jailhouse Rock • Oh, Pretty Woman • Peggy Sue • Runaway • Wake Up Little Susie.

00702572 Book/CD Pack $14.99

6. CHRISTMAS SONGS

Have Yourself a Merry Little Christmas • A Holly Jolly Christmas • The Little Drummer Boy • Run Rudolph Run • Santa Claus Is Comin' to Town • Silver and Gold • Sleigh Ride • Winter Wonderland.

00101879 Book/CD Pack......... $14.99

7. BLUES SONGS FOR BEGINNERS

Come On (Part 1) • Double Trouble • Gangster of Love • I'm Ready • Let Me Love You Baby • Mary Had a Little Lamb • San-Ho-Zay • T-Bone Shuffle.

00103235 Book/
            Online Audio..........$17.99

9. ROCK SONGS FOR BEGINNERS

Are You Gonna Be My Girl • Buddy Holly • Everybody Hurts • In Bloom • Otherside • The Rock Show • Santa Monica • When I Come Around.

00103255 Book/CD Pack.....$14.99

10. GREEN DAY

Basket Case • Boulevard of Broken Dreams • Good Riddance (Time of Your Life) • Holiday • Longview • 21 Guns • Wake Me up When September Ends • When I Come Around.

00122322 Book/
            Online Audio $16.99

11. NIRVANA

All Apologies • Come As You Are • Heart Shaped Box • Lake of Fire • Lithium • The Man Who Sold the World • Rape Me • Smells Like Teen Spirit.

00122325 Book/
            Online Audio $17.99

13. AC/DC

Back in Black • Dirty Deeds Done Dirt Cheap • For Those About to Rock (We Salute You) • Hells Bells • Highway to Hell • Rock and Roll Ain't Noise Pollution • T.N.T. • You Shook Me All Night Long.

14042895 Book/
            Online Audio........ $17.99

14. JIMI HENDRIX – SMASH HITS

All Along the Watchtower • Can You See Me • Crosstown Traffic • Fire • Foxey Lady • Hey Joe • Manic Depression • Purple Haze • Red House • Remember • Stone Free • The Wind Cries Mary.

00130591 Book/
            Online Audio........$24.99

HAL•LEONARD®

www.halleonard.com

Prices, contents, and availability subject to change without notice.

EASY GUITAR WITH NOTES & TAB

This series features simplified arrangements with notes, tab, chord charts, and strum and pick patterns.

MIXED FOLIOS

00702287	Acoustic	$19.99
00702002	Acoustic Rock Hits for Easy Guitar	$15.99
00702166	All-Time Best Guitar Collection	$19.99
00702232	Best Acoustic Songs for Easy Guitar	$16.99
00119835	Best Children's Songs	$16.99
00703055	The Big Book of Nursery Rhymes & Children's Songs	$16.99
00698978	Big Christmas Collection	$19.99
00702394	Bluegrass Songs for Easy Guitar	$15.99
00289632	Bohemian Rhapsody	$19.99
00703387	Celtic Classics	$16.99
00224808	Chart Hits of 2016-2017	$14.99
00267383	Chart Hits of 2017-2018	$14.99
00334293	Chart Hits of 2019-2020	$16.99
00403479	Chart Hits of 2021-2022	$16.99
00702149	Children's Christian Songbook	$9.99
00702028	Christmas Classics	$8.99
00101779	Christmas Guitar	$14.99
00702141	Classic Rock	$8.95
00159642	Classical Melodies	$12.99
00253933	Disney/Pixar's Coco	$16.99
00702203	CMT's 100 Greatest Country Songs	$34.99
00702283	The Contemporary Christian Collection	$16.99

00196954	Contemporary Disney	$19.99
00702239	Country Classics for Easy Guitar	$24.99
00702257	Easy Acoustic Guitar Songs	$17.99
00702041	Favorite Hymns for Easy Guitar	$12.99
00222701	Folk Pop Songs	$17.99
00126894	Frozen	$14.99
00333922	Frozen 2	$14.99
00702286	Glee	$16.99
00702160	The Great American Country Songbook	$19.99
00702148	Great American Gospel for Guitar	$14.99
00702050	Great Classical Themes for Easy Guitar	$9.99
00275088	The Greatest Showman	$17.99
00148030	Halloween Guitar Songs	$14.99
00702273	Irish Songs	$14.99
00192503	Jazz Classics for Easy Guitar	$16.99
00702275	Jazz Favorites for Easy Guitar	$17.99
00702274	Jazz Standards for Easy Guitar	$19.99
00702162	Jumbo Easy Guitar Songbook	$24.99
00232285	La La Land	$16.99
00702258	Legends of Rock	$14.99
00702189	MTV's 100 Greatest Pop Songs	$34.99
00702272	1950s Rock	$16.99
00702271	1960s Rock	$16.99
00702270	1970s Rock	$24.99
00702269	1980s Rock	$16.99

00702268	1990s Rock	$24.99
00369043	Rock Songs for Kids	$14.99
00109725	Once	$14.99
00702187	Selections from O Brother Where Art Thou?	$19.99
00702178	100 Songs for Kids	$16.99
00702515	Pirates of the Caribbean	$17.99
00702125	Praise and Worship for Guitar	$14.99
00287930	Songs from *A Star Is Born, The Greatest Showman, La La Land*, and More Movie Musicals	$16.99
00702285	Southern Rock Hits	$12.99
00156420	Star Wars Music	$16.99
00121535	30 Easy Celtic Guitar Solos	$16.99
00244654	Top Hits of 2017	$14.99
00283786	Top Hits of 2018	$14.99
00302269	Top Hits of 2019	$14.99
00355779	Top Hits of 2020	$14.99
00374083	Top Hits of 2021	$16.99
00702294	Top Worship Hits	$17.99
00702255	VH1's 100 Greatest Hard Rock Songs	$34.99
00702175	VH1's 100 Greatest Songs of Rock and Roll	$34.99
00702253	Wicked	$12.99

ARTIST COLLECTIONS

00702267	AC/DC for Easy Guitar	$16.99
00156221	Adele – 25	$16.99
00396889	Adele – 30	$19.99
00702040	Best of the Allman Brothers	$16.99
00702865	J.S. Bach for Easy Guitar	$15.99
00702169	Best of The Beach Boys	$16.99
00702292	The Beatles — 1	$22.99
00125796	Best of Chuck Berry	$16.99
00702201	The Essential Black Sabbath	$15.99
00702250	blink-182 — Greatest Hits	$17.99
02501615	Zac Brown Band — The Foundation	$17.99
02501621	Zac Brown Band — You Get What You Give	$16.99
00702043	Best of Johnny Cash	$17.99
00702090	Eric Clapton's Best	$16.99
00702086	Eric Clapton — from the Album Unplugged	$17.99
00702202	The Essential Eric Clapton	$17.99
00702053	Best of Patsy Cline	$17.99
00222697	Very Best of Coldplay – 2nd Edition	$17.99
00702229	The Very Best of Creedence Clearwater Revival	$16.99
00702145	Best of Jim Croce	$16.99
00702278	Crosby, Stills & Nash	$12.99
14042809	Bob Dylan	$15.99
00702276	Fleetwood Mac — Easy Guitar Collection	$17.99
00139462	The Very Best of Grateful Dead	$16.99
00702136	Best of Merle Haggard	$16.99
00702227	Jimi Hendrix — Smash Hits	$19.99
00702288	Best of Hillsong United	$12.99
00702236	Best of Antonio Carlos Jobim	$15.99

00702245	Elton John — Greatest Hits 1970–2002	$19.99
00129855	Jack Johnson	$17.99
00702204	Robert Johnson	$16.99
00702234	Selections from Toby Keith — 35 Biggest Hits	$12.95
00702003	Kiss	$16.99
00702216	Lynyrd Skynyrd	$17.99
00702182	The Essential Bob Marley	$16.99
00146081	Maroon 5	$14.99
00121925	Bruno Mars – Unorthodox Jukebox	$12.99
00702248	Paul McCartney — All the Best	$14.99
00125484	The Best of MercyMe	$12.99
00702209	Steve Miller Band — Young Hearts (Greatest Hits)	$12.95
00124167	Jason Mraz	$15.99
00702096	Best of Nirvana	$16.99
00702211	The Offspring — Greatest Hits	$17.99
00138026	One Direction	$17.99
00702030	Best of Roy Orbison	$17.99
00702144	Best of Ozzy Osbourne	$14.99
00702279	Tom Petty	$17.99
00102911	Pink Floyd	$17.99
00702139	Elvis Country Favorites	$19.99
00702293	The Very Best of Prince	$19.99
00699415	Best of Queen for Guitar	$16.99
00109279	Best of R.E.M.	$14.99
00702208	Red Hot Chili Peppers — Greatest Hits	$17.99
00198960	The Rolling Stones	$17.99
00174793	The Very Best of Santana	$16.99
00702196	Best of Bob Seger	$16.99
00146046	Ed Sheeran	$17.99

00702252	Frank Sinatra — Nothing But the Best	$12.99
00702010	Best of Rod Stewart	$17.99
00702049	Best of George Strait	$17.99
00702259	Taylor Swift for Easy Guitar	$15.99
00359800	Taylor Swift – Easy Guitar Anthology	$24.99
00702260	Taylor Swift — Fearless	$14.99
00139727	Taylor Swift — 1989	$19.99
00115960	Taylor Swift — Red	$16.99
00253667	Taylor Swift — Reputation	$17.99
00702290	Taylor Swift — Speak Now	$16.99
00232849	Chris Tomlin Collection – 2nd Edition	$14.99
00702226	Chris Tomlin — See the Morning	$12.95
00148643	Train	$14.99
00702427	U2 — 18 Singles	$19.99
00702108	Best of Stevie Ray Vaughan	$17.99
00279005	The Who	$14.99
00702123	Best of Hank Williams	$15.99
00194548	Best of John Williams	$14.99
00702228	Neil Young — Greatest Hits	$17.99
00119133	Neil Young — Harvest	$14.99

Prices, contents and availability subject to change without notice.

HAL•LEONARD®

Visit Hal Leonard online at **halleonard.com**